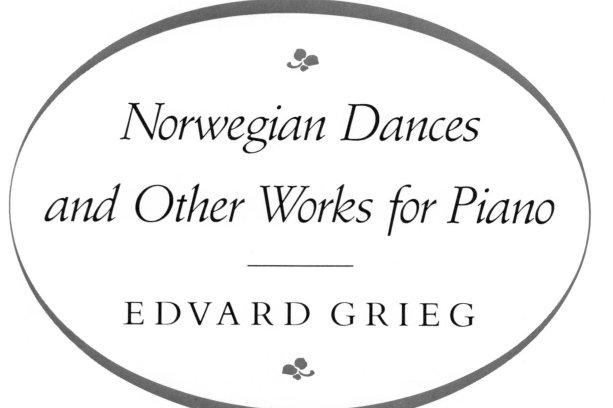

Norwegian Dances
and Other Works for Piano

EDVARD GRIEG

DOVER PUBLICATIONS, INC., NEW YORK

Published in Canada by General Publishing Company, Ltd.,
30 Lesmill Road, Don Mills, Toronto, Ontario.
Published in the United Kingdom by Constable and Company, Ltd.,
3 The Lanchesters, 162–164 Fulham Palace Road, London W6 9ER.

This Dover edition, first published in 1991, is a republication
of portions of Volumes II and III of *Werke für Klavier zu 2 Händen*
and the complete *Slåtter (Norwegische Bauerntänze)*, all originally
published by C. F. Peters, Leipzig, n.d.

Manufactured in the United States of America
Dover Publications, Inc.
31 East 2nd Street
Mineola, N.Y. 11501

Library of Congress Cataloging-in-Publication Data

Grieg, Edvard, 1843–1907.
    [Piano music. Selections]
    Norwegian dances and other works : for piano / Edvard Grieg.
       p.   of music.
    Reprint of works originally published by C. F. Peters in v. 2–3 of
Werke für Klavier zu 2 Händen and the complete Slåtter.
    Contents: Twenty-five Norwegian folk songs and dances : op.
17 — Scenes of country life : op. 19 — Ballade in the form of
variations on a Norwegian folk song : op. 24 — Improvisata on
Norwegian folk tunes : op. 29 — Four Norwegian dances : arr. of
op. 35 — Valses-caprices : arr. of op. 37 — Prayer and temple
dance from Olav Trygvason : arr. from op. 50 — Three orchestral
pieces from Sigurd Jorsalfar : arr. of op. 56 — Two Nordic melo-
dies : arr. of op. 63 — Nineteen Norwegian folk tunes : op. 66 —
Slåtter = Norwegian peasant dances : op. 72.
    ISBN 0-486-26669-9
    1. Piano music.   2. Piano music, Arranged.   I. Title.   II. Title:
Norwegian dances.
M22.G84D8   1991   91-9878
                                             CIP
                                               M

CONTENTS

Twenty-five Norwegian Folk Songs and Dances,
Op. 17

Norske folkeviser og dandse—25 nordische Tänze und Volksweisen

I. Springar

Springtanz

II. The Young Man Asked His Maiden

Ungersvenden han bad sin pige—Der Jüngling

III. Springar

Springtanz

IV. Nils Tallefjorn, Proud Fellow

Niels Tallefjorn den kaute karen—Niels Tallefjoren

V. Jølstring

Tanz aus Jölster

VI. Wedding Tune
Brulåt—Brautlied

VII. Halling

VIII. Oh, the Pig Had a Snout

Å grisen hadde eit tryne—Grisen

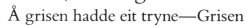

IX. When My Eyes

Når mit øie—Geistliches Lied

X. Ole Once in Anger

Å Ole engang i sinde—Lied des Freiers

XI. On the Dovrefjeld in Norway

På Dovrefjeld i Norge—Heldenlied

XII. Solfager and the Snake King

Solfager og Ormekongen—Solfager und der Würmerkönig

XIII. Wedding Recessional March

Reiselåt—Reiselied

XIV. I Sing with a Sorrowful Heart

Jeg sjunger med et sorrigfuldt hjerte—Trauergesang

XV. The Last Saturday Night

Den sidste laurdags kvelden—Die letzte Sonnabendnacht

XVI. I Know of a Little Maiden

Je veit ei lita jente—Ich weiss ein kleines Mädchen

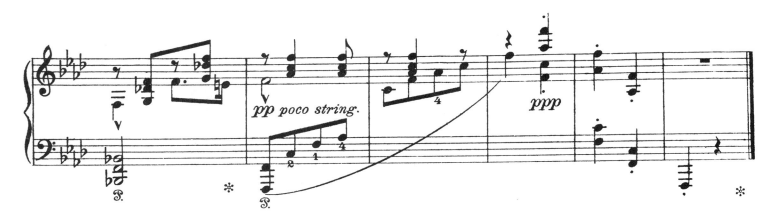

XVII. The Gadfly Said to the Fly

Å kleggen han sa no te flugga si—Die Bremse und die Fliege

XVIII. Stumping Dance
Stabbe-Låtten—Humoristischer Tanz

XIX. Hølje Dale

XX. Halling

XXI. The Woman from Setesdal

XXII. Cattle Call

So lokka me over den myra—Kuhreigen

XXIII. Did You See Anything of My Wife?

Såg du nokke kjæringa mi—Bauernlied

XIV. Wedding Tune

Brulåt—Brautlied

XXV. The Ravens' Wedding in Kråkalund

Ravna bryllupet i Kråkalund—Rabenhochzeit

Scenes of Country Life, Op. 19

Folkelivsbilleder—Aus dem Volksleben

I. Mountain Dance

Fjeldslåt—Auf den Bergen

II. The Bridal Procession Passes
Brudefølget drar forbi—Norwegischer Brautzug im Vorüberziehen

*) 2ª volta una corda.

III. From the Carnival

Fra Karnevalet—Aus dem Karneval

Ballade in the Form of Variations
on a Norwegian Folk Song, Op. 24
Ballade i form av variasjoner over en norsk folkevise—Ballade

Un poco Allegro e alla burla

Meno Allegro e maestoso

Improvisata on Norwegian Folk Tunes, Op. 29

Improvisata over norske folkeviser—
Improvisata über zwei norwegische Volksweisen

I.

Allegro

II.

Improvisata on Norwegian Folk Tunes

Improvisata on Norwegian Folk Tunes

Four Norwegian Dances, arr. of Op. 35

Norwegische Tänze

I.

II.

Allegretto tranquillo e grazioso. ♩ = 76

III.

IV.

Coda
Meno Presto ♩=100

Valses–Caprices, arr. of Op. 37

Walzer-Capricen

I.

II.

Poco meno Allegro

Prayer and Temple Dance
from *Olav Trygvason*, arr. from Op. 50
Gebet und Tempeltanz

Three Orchestral Pieces
from *Sigurd Jorsalfar*, arr. of Op. 56
Drei Orchesterstücke aus *Sigurd Jorsalfar*

I. Prelude
Vorspiel

II. Intermezzo (Borghild's Dream)
Intermezzo (Borghilds Traum)

III. Triumphal March
Huldigungsmarsch

Three Pieces from Sigurd Jorsalfar

Maestoso

Two Nordic Melodies, arr. of Op. 63
Zwei nordische Weisen für Streichorchester

I. In Folk Style (melody by Fredrik Due)
Im Volkston

II. Cattle Call and Peasant Dance
Kuhreigen und Bauerntanz

Cattle Call

Peasant Dance

Allegro molto vivace

Allegro moderato

Nineteen Norwegian Folk Tunes, Op. 66

Norske folkeviser—19 norwegische Volksweisen

I. Cattle Call

Kulok—Lockruf

II. It Is the Greatest Folly

Det er den største Dårlighed—Es ist die grösste Torheit

III. A King Ruled in the East

En Konge hersked i Østerland—Ein König herrschte im Morgenland

IV. The Song of Siri Dale
Siri Dale Visen—Die Weise von Siri Dale

V. It Was in My Youth
Det var i min Ungdom—Es war in meiner Jugend

VI. Cattle Call and Lullaby

Lok og Bådnlåt—Lockruf und Kinderlied

VII. Lullaby
Bådnlåt—Wiegenlied

VIII. Cattle Call
Lok—Lockruf

IX. Small Was the Lad

Liten va Guten—Klein war der Bursch

X. Tomorrow You Shall Marry Her

Morgo ska du få gifte deg—Morgen darfst du sie heimführen

XI. There Stood Two Girls

Der stander to Piger—Es stehen zwei Mägdlein

XII. Ranveig

attacca

XIII. A Little Gray Man

En liten grå Man—Ein graues Männlein

XIV. In Ola Valley, in Ola Lake

I Ola-Dalom, i Ola-Kjønn—Im Olatal, im Olasee

XV. Lullaby

Bådnlåt—Wiegenlied

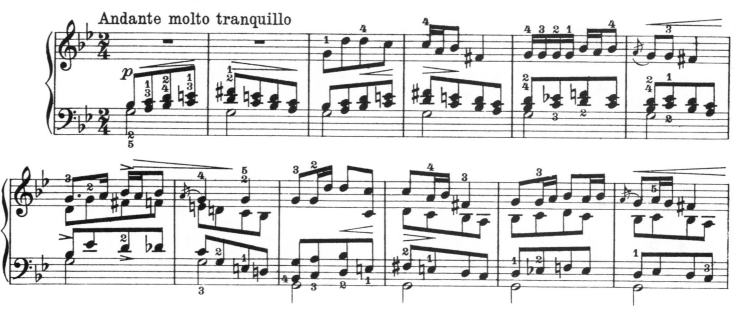

XVI. Our Little Astrid

Ho vesle Astrid vor—Klein Astrid

XVII. Lullaby

Bådnlåt—Wiegenlied

XVIII. I Wander Deep in Thought

Jeg går i tusind Tanker—Gedankenvoll ich wandere

XIX. Gjendine's Lullaby

Gjendines Bådnlåt—Gjendines Wiegenlied

Slåtter (Norwegian Peasant Dances), Op. 72
Slåtter (Norwegische Bauerntänze)

PREFACE.

These Norwegian "Slåtter" ("Slåt" is the usual Norwegian name for the peasant's dance), now for the first time brought before the public in their original form for the violin (or for the so-called Hardanger-fiddle) and re-arranged for the piano, were written down after an old gleeman in Telemarken. Those who can appreciate such music, will be delighted at the originality, the blending of fine, soft gracefulness with sturdy almost uncouth power and untamed wildness as regards melody and more particularly rhythm, contained in them. This music,—which is handed down to us from an age when the culture of the Norwegian peasant was isolated in its solitary mountain-valleys from the outer world, to which fact it owes its whole originality,—bears the stamp of an imagination as daring in its flight as it is peculiar.

My object in arranging the music for the piano was to raise these works of the people to an artistic level, by giving them what I might call a style of musical concord, or bringing them under a system of harmony. Naturally, many of the little embellishments, characteristic of the peasant's fiddle and of their peculiar manner of bowing, cannot be reproduced on the piano, and had accordingly to be left out. On the other hand, by virtue of its manifold dynamic and rhythmic qualities, the piano affords the great advantage of enabling us to avoid a monotonous uniformity, by varying the harmony of repeated passages or parts. I have endeavoured to make myself clear in the lines set forth, in fact, to obtain a definite form. The few passages in which I considered myself authorized as an artist, to add to, or work out the given motives, will easily be found, on comparing my arrangement with the original, written down by Johan Halvorsen, in a manner reliable even for research-work, and published by the same firm.

The "Slåtter" sound a minor third higher, when played on the peasant's fiddle; nevertheless, I have retained the key in which the original is written down, in order to obtain a fuller effect on the piano.

Fovord.

Disse norske „Slåtter" (Slåt er det norske Udtryk for Bondedans) som for förste Gang i Original-optegnelse for Hardangerviolinen og i fri Bearbeidelse for Pianoforte overgives til Offentligheden, er nedskrevet efter en gammel Spillemand i Telemarken. Hvem der har Sans for disse Klange vil henföres af deres store Originalitet, deres Blanding af fin og skjær Ynde med djærv Kraft og utæmmet Vildhed i melodisk, som især i rytmisk Henseende. De bærer Præget af en ligeså dristig, som bizar Fantasi, disse Levninger fra en Tid, da den norske Bondekultur var afstængt fra Udenverdenen i de afsidesliggende Fjelddale og netop derfor har bevaret hele sin Oprindelighed.

Min Opgave ved Overföringen til Pianoet var et Forsög på, gjennem, lad mig kalde det stiliseret Harmonik a hæve disse Folketoner op til et kunstnerisk Niveau Det ligger i Sagens Natur, at Klaveret måtte give Afkald på mange a₁ de små Forsiringer, der bunder i Hardangerfelens Karakter og Bueföringens Ejendommelighed. Til Gjenjæld har Klaveret den store Fordel, gjennem dynamisk og rytmisk Mangfoldighed, samt gjennem ny Harmonisering af Gjentagelserne at kunne undgå en altfor fremtrædende Ensformighed. Jeg har bestræbt mig for at optrække klare, over-skuelige Linjer, overhovedet at skabe en fast Form. De få Steder, hvor jeg holdt det for kunstnerisk berettiget at bygge videre på de foreliggende Motiver, vil man let udfinde ved at sammenligne min Bearbeidelse med den samtidig på samme Forlag udkomne Originaloptegnelse af Johan Halvorsen, der er at betragte som Kildeskrift.

Tiltrods for at Slåtterne på Hardangerfelen klinger en liden Terts höjere, har jeg dog, forat opnå en fyldigere Klavervirkning, valgt at beholde den Toneart, hvori Originalen er optegnet.

Edvard Grieg.

I. Gibøen's Wedding March
Gibøens bruremarsj—Gibøens Brautmarsch

II. Jon Væstafæ's Springar

Jon Væstafæs springdans—Jon Vestafes Springdans

III. Wedding March from Telemark

Bruremarsj fra Telemark—Brautmarsch aus Telemark

Halling from the Gnomes' Hill

This "Halling" is connected with the following legend:

A man, by the name of Brynjuw Olson, had lost a bull. After searching for the animal in the mountains, for several days, he became exhausted and fell asleep. He dreamed that he heard a wondrous strange song. Behind a hill he saw a beautiful maiden; she called to him and said: "Yea! so shalt thou play on the fiddle, Brynjuw Olson, when thou returnest home to wife and child, and yonder, where the mountains disappear, wilt thou find the bull."

Til denne Halling knytter sig fölgende Fortælling:

„En Mand som hed Brynjuv Olson havde mistet en Stut. Han gik og ledte efter den i Fjeldet i flere Dage. Så blev han træt og faldt i Sövn, og hörte i Sövnen en underlig Låt. Bortom en Haug så han ei nögli fin Jente. Jenten sa til ham: „Ja, så ska du spela på Violen, du Brynjuv Olson, når du kjem hejmat til Kjærring og Bon —

og bortæfor Nuten,
der fin du Stuten."

IV. Halling from the Gnomes' Hill*

Haugelåt. Halling—Halling aus dem Hügel

★) Abode of the fairies.

V. The Prillar from Os Parish (Springar)*

Prillaren fra Os prestegjeld. Springdans—
Der Prillar aus dem Kirchenspiel Os. Springdans

*)"**Prillar**", Dance for Prillarhorn (or
Trill-horn), a wind-instrument made
out of a cow's or a goat's horn, and
provided with stops.

VI. Myllarguten's Gangar

Gangar (etter Myllarguten)—Myllargutens Gangar

The Miller's man, or simply "the Miller" was the most celebrated Norwegian Fiddle-player in the middle of the last century.

VII. Røtnams-Knut (Halling)

Allegro moderato, ma vivace. ♩= 100.*)

*) It was necessary to accelerate
the time indicated in the original,
in order to obtain the effect required
in the piano part.

Majore da capo al fine.

VIII. Myllarguten's Wedding March

Bruremarsj (etter Myllarguten)—Myllargutens Brautmarsch

According to a well-known gleeman from Tele-marken, this march is by „the Miller", when Kari broke off her engagement with him, in order to marry another.

Ifölge en bekjendt Spillemand fra Telemar-ken, er denne Marsch komponeret af „Möllargutten" da hans Kjæreste, Kari, sveg ham forat gifte sig med en Anden.

*) Play the appoggiaturas always to-gether with the bass.

**)

IX. Nils Rekve's Halling

Nils Rekves halling

X. Knut Luråsen's Halling I

Knut Luråsens halling I

*) From here on the unison octaves should be played with maximum power.

NB: together — gleichzeitig

XI. Knut Luråsen's Halling II

Knut Luråsens halling II

XII. Myllarguten's Springar

Springdans (etter Myllarguten)—Myllargutens Springdans

XIII. Havar Gibøen's Dream on the Oterholt Bridge (Springar)

Havar Gibøens draum ved Oterholtsbrua. Springdans—
Havar Gibøens Traum an der Oterholtsbrücke. Springdans

XIV. The Goblins' Wedding Procession at Vossevangen (Gangar)

Tussebrureferda på Vossevangen. Gangar—
Die Brautfahrt der Unterirdischen auf Vossevangen. Gangar

XV. The Skuldal Bride (Gangar)

Skuldalsbrura. Gangar—Die Skuldalsbraut. Gangar

The Maidens of Kivledal

In Selljord in Telemarken there is a little valley, called Kivledal. In ancient times, a tiny church stood in this valley. One Sunday, when the community had assembled for mass, loud sounds from the mountain suddenly reverberated through the church. It was the three maidens of Kivledal, the last heathens in the valley, who, while watching their goats on the mountain-slopes, were blowing a "Slåt" on the Trill-horn. The community rushed out of the church and listened enraptured to the wondrous enchanting tones. The parson followed, and called to the maidens, bidding them stop playing; but as they kept on blowing their horns, he raised his hands and anathematised them in the name of God and the Pope. The maidens of Kivledal and their herds were at once changed into stone. And to this day, you can see them standing high up on the mountain-slope, the horn to their mouth and their herds around them. This is the legend of the "Slåt" of the maidens of Kivledal, as preserved by the peasants in the valley, and which they still play on their fiddles. The following "Slåt" is related to this same legend: There are in all three such "Slåtter" (one for each of the maidens), and only that fiddler was considered great who could play all three.

I Selljord i Telemarken ligger en liden Dal som hedder Kivledalen. Der stod i gamle Dage en örliden Kirke. — En Söndag, mens Menigheden var samlet til Messe, klang der med et stærke Toner gjennem Kirken oppe fra Uren. Det var „Kivlemöyerne," de tre sidste Hedninger i Dalen, som gjeted sine Gjeter i Lien og gik og blæste en Slåt på „Trillarhorn." (Det telemarkiske Navn på „Prillarhorn.") Almuen strömmed ud af Kirken og lytted som fjetret til de gribende Toner. Presten fulgte efter, han ropte til „Möyerne," at de skulde holde op og da de blev ved at blæse, löfted han Hånden og lyste dem i Guds og Pavens Bann. I det Samme blev Kivlemöyerne og hele Gjeteflokken til Sten. Og den Dag idag ser man dem stå höjt oppe i Uren, med Hornet for Munden og Gjeterne rundt om sig. — Dette er Kivlemöyernes Slåt, slig som Dalens Bönder har bevaret den og endnu spiller den på sin Hardangerfele. Om den fölgende Slåt gjælder det samme Sagn. Der findes i det Hele tre slige Slåtter og kun den Spillemand gjaldt for Noget, der kunde spille alle tre.

XVI. The Maidens of Kivledal (Springar)

Kivlemøyane. Springdans—Die Mädchen aus dem Kivledal. Springdans

XVII. The Maidens of Kivledal (Gangar)
Kivlemøyane. Gangar—Die Mädchen aus dem Kivledal. Gangar

Dover Piano and Keyboard Editions

THE WELL-TEMPERED CLAVIER: Books I and II, Complete, Johann Sebastian Bach. All 48 preludes and fugues in all major and minor keys. Authoritative Bach-Gesellschaft edition. Explanation of ornaments in English, tempo indications, music corrections. 208pp. 9⅜ × 12¼. 24532-2 Pa. **$8.95**

KEYBOARD MUSIC, J. S. Bach. Bach-Gesellschaft edition. For harpsichord, piano, other keyboard instruments. English Suites, French Suites, Six Partitas, Goldberg Variations, Two-Part Inventions, Three-Part Sinfonias. 312pp. 8⅛ × 11. 22360-4 Pa. **$9.95**

ITALIAN CONCERTO, CHROMATIC FANTASIA AND FUGUE AND OTHER WORKS FOR KEYBOARD, Johann Sebastian Bach. Sixteen of Bach's best-known, most-performed and most-recorded works for the keyboard, reproduced from the authoritative Bach-Gesellschaft edition. 112pp. 9 × 12. 25387-2 Pa. **$5.95**

COMPLETE KEYBOARD TRANSCRIPTIONS OF CONCERTOS BY BAROQUE COMPOSERS, Johann Sebastian Bach. Sixteen concertos by Vivaldi, Telemann and others, transcribed for solo keyboard instruments. Bach-Gesellschaft edition. 128pp. 9⅜ × 12¼. 25529-8 Pa. **$6.95**

ORGAN MUSIC, J. S. Bach. Bach-Gesellschaft edition. 93 works. 6 Trio Sonatas, German Organ Mass, Orgelbüchlein, Six Schubler Chorales, 18 Choral Preludes. 357pp. 8⅛ × 11. 22359-0 Pa. **$12.50**

COMPLETE PRELUDES AND FUGUES FOR ORGAN, Johann Sebastian Bach. All 25 of Bach's complete sets of preludes and fugues (i.e. compositions written as pairs), from the authoritative Bach-Gesellschaft edition. 168pp. 8⅜ × 11. 24816-X Pa. **$7.95**

TOCCATAS, FANTASIAS, PASSACAGLIA AND OTHER WORKS FOR ORGAN, J. S. Bach. Over 20 best-loved works including Toccata and Fugue in D minor, BWV 565; Passacaglia and Fugue in C minor, BWV 582, many more. Bach-Gesellschaft edition. 176pp. 9 × 12. 25403-8 Pa. **$8.95**

TWO- AND THREE-PART INVENTIONS, J. S. Bach. Reproduction of original autograph ms. Edited by Eric Simon. 62pp. 8⅛ × 11. 21982-8 Pa. **$5.95**

THE 36 FANTASIAS FOR KEYBOARD, Georg Philipp Telemann. Graceful compositions by 18th-century master. 1923 Breslauer edition. 80pp. 8⅛ × 11. 25365-1 Pa. **$4.50**

GREAT KEYBOARD SONATAS, Carl Philipp Emanuel Bach. Comprehensive two-volume edition contains 51 sonatas by second, most important son of Johann Sebastian Bach. Originality, rich harmony, delicate workmanship. Authoritative French edition. Total of 384pp. 8⅜ × 11¼. Series I 24853-4 Pa. **$7.95** Series II 24854-2 Pa. **$7.95**

KEYBOARD WORKS/Series One: Ordres I–XIII; Series Two: Ordres XIV–XXVII and Miscellaneous Pieces, François Couperin. Over 200 pieces. Reproduced directly from edition prepared by Johannes Brahms and Friedrich Chrysander. Total of 496pp. 8⅛ × 11. Series I 25795-9 Pa. **$9.95** Series II 25796-7 Pa. **$9.95**

KEYBOARD WORKS FOR SOLO INSTRUMENTS, G. F. Handel. 35 neglected works from Handel's vast oeuvre, originally jotted down as improvisations. Includes Eight Great Suites, others. New sequence. 174pp. 9⅜ × 12¼. 24338-9 Pa. **$7.95**

WORKS FOR ORGAN AND KEYBOARD, Jan Pieterszoon Sweelinck. Nearly all of early Dutch composer's difficult-to-find keyboard works. Chorale variations; toccatas, fantasias; variations on secular, dance tunes. Also, incomplete and/or modified works, plus fantasia by John Bull. 272pp. 9 × 12. 24935-2 Pa. **$10.95**

ORGAN WORKS, Dietrich Buxtehude. Complete organ works of extremely influential pre-Bach composer. Toccatas, preludes, chorales, more. Definitive Breitkopf & Härtel edition. 320pp. 8⅝ × 11¼. (USO) 25682-0 Pa. **$11.95**

THE FUGUES ON THE MAGNIFICAT FOR ORGAN OR KEYBOARD, Johann Pachelbel. 94 pieces representative of Pachelbel's magnificent contribution to keyboard composition; can be played on the organ, harpsichord or piano. 100pp. 9 × 12. (USO) 25037-7 Pa. **$5.95**

MY LADY NEVELLS BOOKE OF VIRGINAL MUSIC, William Byrd. 42 compositions in modern notation from 1591 ms. For any keyboard instrument. 245pp. 8⅛ × 11. 22246-2 Pa. **$9.95**

ELIZABETH ROGERS HIR VIRGINALL BOOKE, edited with calligraphy by Charles J. F. Cofone. All 112 pieces from noted 1656 manuscript, most never before published. Composers include Thomas Brewer, William Byrd, Orlando Gibbons, etc. 125pp. 9 × 12. 23138-0 Pa. **$8.95**

THE FITZWILLIAM VIRGINAL BOOK, edited by J. Fuller Maitland, W. B. Squire. Famous early 17th-century collection of keyboard music, 300 works by Morley, Byrd, Bull, Gibbons, etc. Modern notation. Total of 938pp. 8⅜ × 11. Two-vol. set. 21068-5, 21069-3 Pa. **$27.90**

GREAT KEYBOARD SONATAS, Series I and Series II, Domenico Scarlatti. 78 of the most popular sonatas reproduced from the G. Ricordi edition edited by Alessandro Longo. Total of 320pp. 8⅝ × 11¼. Series I 24996-4 Pa. **$6.95** Series II 25003-2 Pa. **$6.95**

SONATAS AND FANTASIES FOR THE PIANO, W. A. Mozart, edited by Nathan Broder. Finest, most accurate edition, based on autographs and earliest editions. 19 sonatas, plus Fantasy and Fugue in C, K.394, Fantasy in C Minor, K.396, Fantasy in D Minor, K.397. 352pp. 9 × 12. (USO) 25417-8 Pa. **$14.95**

COMPLETE PIANO SONATAS, Joseph Haydn. 52 sonatas reprinted from authoritative Breitkopf & Härtel edition. Extremely clear and readable; ample space for notes, analysis. 464pp. 9⅜ × 12¼. 24726-0 Pa. **$9.95** 24727-9 Pa. **$9.95**

BAGATELLES, RONDOS AND OTHER SHORTER WORKS FOR PIANO, Ludwig van Beethoven. Most popular and most performed shorter works, including Rondo a capriccio in G and Andante in F. Breitkopf & Härtel edition. 128pp. 9⅜ × 12¼. 25392-9 Pa. **$6.95**

COMPLETE VARIATIONS FOR SOLO PIANO, Ludwig van Beethoven. Contains all 21 sets of Beethoven's piano variations, including the extremely popular *Diabelli Variations, Op. 120.* 240pp. 9⅜ × 12¼. 25188-8 Pa. **$9.95**

COMPLETE PIANO SONATAS, Ludwig van Beethoven. All sonatas in fine Schenker edition, with fingering, analytical material. One of best modern editions. 615pp. 9 × 12. Two-vol. set. (USO) 23134-8, 23135-6 Pa. **$21.90**

COMPLETE SONATAS FOR PIANOFORTE SOLO, Franz Schubert. All 15 sonatas. Breitkopf and Härtel edition. 293pp. 9⅜ × 12¼. 22647-6 Pa. **$10.95**

DANCES FOR SOLO PIANO, Franz Schubert. Over 350 waltzes, minuets, landler, ecossaises, other charming, melodic dance compositions reprinted from the authoritative Breitkopf & Härtel edition. 192pp. 9⅜ × 12¼. 26107-7 Pa. **$8.95**

Available from your music dealer or write for **free** *Music Catalog to*
Dover Publications, Inc., Dept. MUBI, 31 East 2nd Street, Mineola, N.Y. 11501.

Dover Chamber Music Scores

COMPLETE SUITES FOR UNACCOMPANIED CELLO AND SONATAS FOR VIOLA DA GAMBA, Johann Sebastian Bach. Bach-Gesellschaft edition of the six cello suites (BWV 1007–1012) and three sonatas (BWV 1027–1029), commonly played today on the cello. 112pp. 9⅜ × 12¼. 25641-3 Pa. **$6.95**

WORKS FOR VIOLIN, Johann Sebastian Bach. Complete Sonatas and Partitas for Unaccompanied Violin; Six Sonatas for Violin and Clavier. Bach-Gesellschaft edition. 158pp. 9⅜ × 12¼. 23683-8 Pa. **$6.95**

COMPLETE STRING QUARTETS, Wolfgang A. Mozart. Breitkopf & Härtel edition. All 23 string quartets plus alternate slow movement to K.156. Study score. 277pp. 9⅜ × 12¼. 22372-8 Pa. **$10.95**

COMPLETE STRING QUINTETS, Wolfgang Amadeus Mozart. All the standard-instrumentation string quintets, plus String Quintet in C Minor, K.406; Quintet with Horn or Second Cello, K.407; and Clarinet Quintet, K.581. Breitkopf & Härtel edition. Study score. 181pp. 9⅜ × 12¼. 23603-X Pa. **$7.95**

STRING QUARTETS, OPP. 20 and 33, COMPLETE, Joseph Haydn. Complete reproductions of the 12 masterful quartets (six each) of Opps. 20 and 33—in the reliable Eulenburg edition. 272pp. 8⅜ × 11¼. 24852-6 Pa. **$9.95**

STRING QUARTETS, OPP. 42, 50 and 54, Joseph Haydn. Complete reproductions of Op. 42 in D minor; Op. 50, Nos. 1–6 ("Prussian Quartets") and Op. 54, Nos. 1–3. Reliable Eulenburg edition. 224pp. 8⅜ × 11¼. 24262-5 Pa. **$8.95**

TWELVE STRING QUARTETS, Joseph Haydn. 12 often-performed works: Op. 55, Nos. 1–3 (including *Razor*); Op. 64, Nos. 1–6; Op. 71, Nos. 1–3. Definitive Eulenburg edition. 288pp. 8⅜ × 11¼. 23933-0 Pa. **$8.95**

ELEVEN LATE STRING QUARTETS, Joseph Haydn. Complete reproductions of Op. 74, Nos. 1–3; Op. 76, Nos. 1–6; and Op. 77, Nos. 1 and 2. Definitive Eulenburg edition. Full-size study score. 320pp. 8⅜ × 11¼. 23753-2 Pa. **$10.95**

COMPLETE STRING QUARTETS, Ludwig van Beethoven. Breitkopf & Härtel edition. Six quartets of Opus 18; three quartets of Opus 59; Opera 74, 95, 127, 130, 131, 132, 135 and Grosse Fuge. Study score. 434pp. 9⅜ × 12¼. 22361-2 Pa. **$14.95**

SIX GREAT PIANO TRIOS IN FULL SCORE, Ludwig van Beethoven. Definitive Breitkopf & Härtel edition of Beethoven's Piano Trios Nos. 1–6 including the "Ghost" and the "Archduke". 224pp. 9⅜ × 12¼. 25398-8 Pa. **$9.95**

COMPLETE CHAMBER MUSIC FOR STRINGS, Franz Schubert. Reproduced from famous Breitkopf & Härtel edition: Quintet in C Major (1828), 15 quartets and two trios for violin(s), viola, and violincello. Study score. 348pp. 9 × 12. 21463-X Pa. **$11.95**

COMPLETE CHAMBER MUSIC FOR PIANOFORTE AND STRINGS, Franz Schubert. Breitkopf & Härtel edition. *Trout*, Quartet in F Major, and trios for piano, violin, cello. Study score. 192pp. 9 × 12. 21527-X Pa. **$8.95**

CHAMBER WORKS FOR PIANO AND STRINGS, Felix Mendelssohn. Eleven of the composer's best known works in the genre—duos, trios, quartets and a sextet—reprinted from authoritative Breitkopf & Härtel edition. 384pp. 9⅜ × 12¼. 26117-4 Pa. **$15.95**

COMPLETE CHAMBER MUSIC FOR STRINGS, Felix Mendelssohn. All of Mendelssohn's chamber music: Octet, Two Quintets, Six Quartets, and Four Pieces for String Quartet. (Nothing with piano is included). Complete works edition (1874-7). Study score. 283pp. 9⅜ × 12¼. 23679-X Pa. **$11.95**

CHAMBER MUSIC OF ROBERT SCHUMANN, edited by Clara Schumann. Superb collection of three trios, four quartets, and piano quintet. Breitkopf & Härtel edition. 288pp. 9⅜ × 12¼. 24101-7 Pa. **$9.95**

COMPLETE SONATAS FOR SOLO INSTRUMENT AND PIANO, Johannes Brahms. All seven sonatas—three for violin, two for cello and two for clarinet (or viola)—reprinted from the authoritative Breitkopf & Härtel edition. 208pp. 9 × 12. 26091-7 Pa. **$10.95**

COMPLETE CHAMBER MUSIC FOR STRINGS AND CLARINET QUINTET, Johannes Brahms. Vienna Gesellschaft der Musikfreunde edition of all quartets, quintets, and sextet without piano. Study edition. 262pp. 8⅜ × 11¼. 21914-3 Pa. **$8.95**

QUINTET AND QUARTETS FOR PIANO AND STRINGS, Johannes Brahms. Full scores of *Quintet in F Minor*, Op. 34; *Quartet in G Minor*, Op. 25; *Quartet in A Major*, Op. 26; *Quartet in C Minor*, Op. 60. Breitkopf & Härtel edition. 298pp. 9 × 12. 24900-X Pa. **$11.95**

COMPLETE PIANO TRIOS, Johannes Brahms. All five piano trios in the definitive Breitkopf & Härtel edition. 288pp. 9 × 12. 25769-X Pa. **$10.95**

CHAMBER WORKS FOR PIANO AND STRINGS, Antonín Dvořák. Society editions of the F Minor and Dumky piano trios, D Major and E-flat Major piano quartets and A Major piano quintet. 352pp. 8⅜ × 11¼. (USO) 25663-4 Pa. **$13.95**

FIVE LATE STRING QUARTETS, Antonín Dvořák. Treasury of Czech master's finest chamber works: Nos. 10, 11, 12, 13, 14. Reliable Simrock editions. 282pp. 8⅜ × 11. 25135-7 Pa. **$9.95**

STRING QUARTETS BY DEBUSSY AND RAVEL/Claude Debussy: Quartet in G Minor, Op. 10/Maurice Ravel: Quartet in F Major, Claude Debussy and Maurice Ravel. Authoritative one-volume edition of two influential masterpieces noted for individuality, delicate and subtle beauties. 112pp. 8⅜ × 11. (USO) 25231-0 Pa. **$5.95**

---

*Available from your music dealer or write for **free** Music Catalog to Dover Publications, Inc., Dept. MUBI, 31 East 2nd Street, Mineola, N.Y. 11501.*